Dedication

I dedicate this book to my children,
Beth, Claire and Jessica.
They share my fascination with these furry friends
and it is their questions that I am answering here.
Also for Mike, who would have been as
entranced by alpacas as we are.
X

Published by Jane Pyne
Publishing partner: Paragon Publishing, Rothersthorpe
First published 2009
© Jane Pyne 2009
The rights of Jane Pyne to be identified as the author of this work have been asserted by her in accordance with the Copyright, Designs and Patents Act of 1988.
All rights reserved; no part of this publication may be reproduced, stored in a retrieval system, or transmitted in any form or by any means, electronic, mechanical, photocopying, recording or otherwise without the prior written consent of the publisher or a licence permitting copying in the UK issued by the Copyright Licensing Agency Ltd, 90 Tottenham Court Road, London W1P 9HE.

Condition of Sale

This book is sold subject to the condition that it shall not, by way of trade or otherwise, be lent, resold, hired out or otherwise circulated in any form of binding or cover other than that in which it is published and without a similar condition including this condition being imposed on the subsequent purchaser.
No part of this book may be reproduced or transmitted in any form or by any means electronic, chemical or mechanical, including photocopying, any information storage or retrieval system without a licence or other permission in writing from the copyright owners. Reviewers are welcome to quote brief passages should they wish.
ISBN 978-1-899820-76-4
Book design, layout and production management by Into Print
www.intoprint.net

Printed and bound in UK and USA by Lightning Source

Contents	Page	Contents	Page
First Arrivals	4	Breeding for Next Year	14
Alpaca Care	5	Showing Off!	15
Diet	7	Shearing	18
Springtime!	10	Summertime!	19
Sometimes When You're Lucky...!	11	Wintertime!	20
		What's it all For?	21
Alpacas as Mums	12	Alpaca Facts	22
Occasionally Things go Wrong...	13	Glossary	24
		About the Author	26

First Arrivals

Our journey and learning together began here.
The first Tudor Cottage Alpacas arrived in 2008 and were soon very much a part of our world.
Their care and well-being became extremely important and in this book I plan to share with you a little of what happens on a small alpaca farm in the UK.
These gentle, quietly humming creatures are endearing animals and I consider myself to have been fortunate to have found them. My children and those of others enjoy them very much. I hope you will too.

Alpaca Care

Alpacas are generally quite hardy animals. They are from an environment which is extremely harsh to live in. In the Uk most of the care they require from their owners or breeders is fairly simple. It is in the owners' interest as well as the animals to ensure that they are properly looked after and their health is good. If they are in poor condition they will not produce as good **fibre** and they will not reproduce as reliably for the breeder. This is not good for anybody.

The basic care of alpacas will usually be carried out by the breeder. This care will include injections to protect them from various diseases. Alpacas can suffer from many diseases common in sheep and cattle so need similar treatment. Like most animals, they can also suffer from parasites inside them which need treating if they are to remain healthy. This is very much like your pet dog or cat needing a tablet to protect them from worms.

The first sign of ill health is often a loss of weight so breeders will keep a record of their animals' weights.

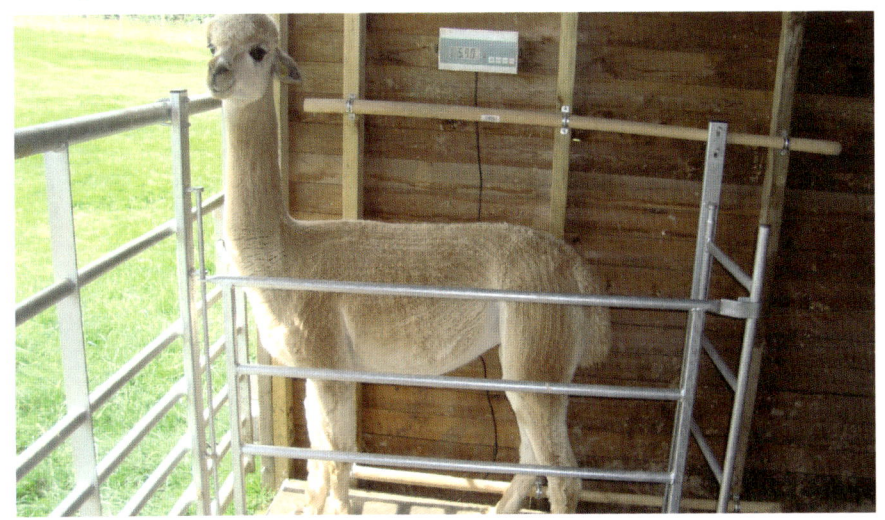

Misty being weighed in the small pen for handling them.

Living with alpacas — 5

In the UK alpacas can also benefit from some vitamin injections. This is mainly to give them a little bit extra vitamin D. This vitamin is produced in the body when there is sunshine. In South America alpacas have more sunshine than in the UK so they need an extra boost here. This vitamin help to keep their bones strong and avoid a condition called **rickets** which causes bones to soften and form incorrectly.

The other regular care for alpacas involves keeping their feet in good condition. Alpacas have soft padded feet with two toes. These toes have nails on them which need to be kept trimmed. This usually only needs doing a couple of time a year if they are not worn down by hard ground. Each individual is different and some will have toe nails that grow more quickly than others. The shearer will check the alpacas nails when he comes and in between the breeder will keep an eye on them. They can be cut with clippers very like garden secateurs.

Living with alpacas — 6

Diet

Alpacas don't need a lot of special foods. Their main diet is grass so if you have adequate grazing for your alpacas their need for anything else is not very great. They do need to have hay available to them but will often not eat large amounts. As the grass in this country is quite different to the deep rooted plants of their home land the mineral contents are different too. The other food they are given, in pellets, is mainly minerals to make sure they get everything they need.
They also need to have access to fresh water at all times, as with other livestock.

Little Rosie is learning about hayracks from Auntie Misty

Baby alpacas are called **crias** and they will learn to copy their mums eating when still quite small. They will begin to graze and nibble on hay and pellets at just a couple of weeks of age.

Elspeth getting to grips with grazing aged 2 weeks.

Alpacas have a complicated stomach a bit like cows. They have 3 compartments in their stomachs and are called **ruminants**. This means that food goes into one part of the stomach when they eat it but they will then bring it back to chew again later. It then goes to a different compartment. This enables them to get more goodness from it and this is called 'chewing the cud'. Healthy adults should spend a lot of their relaxing time chewing the cud. **Crias** begin chewing their cud or 'cudding' when they are a few weeks old.

When alpacas are sitting chewing their cud they will generally be in the **cush** position. This is sitting with all their legs tucked under them. They will sit and chew, sometimes dozing a little but some of the herd will be keeping a look out. If one sees

Amaia and her daughter, Elspeth chewing the cud.

something they are nervous about they will soon have the attention of their friends.

Sometimes, if an alpaca feels threatened or stressed and has no space to run, they will go down into a **cush**. This is quite different to the relaxed, cudding alpaca and not something that owners like to see too often. Some individuals will **cush** when you are trying to give injections, for example.

Springtime!

With the arrival of Spring most alpacas and their breeders are preparing for the new **crias**. In the UK it is common for breeders to try to plan it so that their **crias** are born between about April and late September. This is to avoid having very young babies in the colder and wetter months of the year.

As the females can vary quite a lot in exactly how long they will be pregnant, it is difficult to know just when your new arrivals will put in an appearance. The mum might **calve** any time from 10 ½ to 12 months of **gestation**. Fortunately, they do
usually **calve** during the daytime. We think this is because in the Andes, where they come from, they want their babies to be able to run away from danger by the time night falls. Wild lynx are one of the natural predators there and a small **cria**
is vulnerable if it can't move with the herd.

Some people say their alpacas hum more before giving birth, as if talking to their baby.

Even if you look out for clues that they might **calve** soon, you often come back after a couple of hours to find the mum and new baby already there. Perhaps they prefer to be in private!

The **cria** will usually be up very quickly and feeding from mum within a couple of hours of birth.

Sometimes when you're lucky…!

Aunties looking on at Elspeth's birth

This is after about 10 minutes

The cria usually drops out very quickly now

Elspeth is about 2 hours old here.

Living with alpacas — 11

Alpacas as Mums

Alpacas are wonderful mothers. They are generally very calm with one another's **crias** and are happiest when close to the rest of the herd. Although they only have one baby of their own they will graze and rest with other babies too and act as 'aunties'. Even an orphan is generally under no threat from the adults in the herd. The **crias** will have milk from their mums for about the first six months. At this point most breeders will separate them from their mums. This is called weaning.

A brand new Richard is having some milk from mum, Martina.

Micah with her cria, Peggy and playing auntie to Richard.

Living with alpacas — 12

Occasionally things go wrong...

Unfortunately things don't always go to plan. Sadly, with any livestock, there will be times when an animal will die for some reason. The vet can sometimes help to save an ill animal, but this is not always possible.

If a breeder loses a female of breeding age, it is likely that she will either be pregnant or have a **cria**. It is a sad fact that this will sometime result in both mother and **cria** dying. It is very unusual for an alpaca to 'adopt' another **cria**.

Sometimes, with some luck, a young orphaned **cria** will survive being raised on a bottle by the breeder.

Here I am feeding our little orphan, Rosie. She's about 6 weeks old here.

Living with alpacas — 13

Breeding for Next Year

Just a few weeks after calving the females will be ready to mate again in order to become pregnant with next year's **crias**. At this time the breeder will bring a male and female together and if the female is ready to mate she will sit down. The breeder will check a week or two later to see if the female is pregnant. They call this 'spit-offs'! This is because if you put a male in with a pregnant female she will tell him to leave her alone by spitting at him!
It is also possible to check a pregnancy after about 60 days using an ultrasound scan – just like a human being.

A visit from a very beautiful stud to mate with our Annie.

Living with alpacas

Showing off!!

During the summer months many breeders will take some of their animals to shows. There are many agricultural shows and county shows around the UK and some of these will have classes for alpacas. There are also shows organised by the British Alpaca Society and regional events. These shows are an opportunity for breeders to let other breeders, and those possibly looking to buy animals, see how good their animals are. Each breeder will be aiming to improve their **fibre** production in some way. If they get rosettes in the shows they know (and so do other people!) that they must be doing something right.

This is Hope after her ring success.

The judge will look at the way the animals move, and check that their body shape is as it should be. The breeder will need to walk them around a ring on a halter and lead. They will have trained the alpaca for this at home. However, most alpacas will not be used to seeing all the strange sights and people. The judge will also check their teeth to make sure there are no faults which they might pass on to the **crias**. This would suggest that the animal was not a good one to breed with and therefore not a prize winner.

Bessie is being walked here for a show and then showing the judge her teeth. What a good girl!!

Living with alpacas — 16

After that they will have a very close look at their fleece and look at how well it is growing. They want the fleece to be nice and thick over the body and to continue being thick as far as possible up the neck and down the legs. They will look at individual **fibres** from the fleece to see how fine they are and they will compare the softness of the entrants. They will also look at the **crimp** in the fleece. This is a little wave that runs along the length of the **staple**.

The alpacas often attract a lot of attention from the public as they are a little unusual.

Bessie continues to be examined in the ring.

Living with alpacas

Shearing

There are two types of alpaca. **Huacayas** look a little like fuzzy teddy bears and **suris** have tassle like locks of fleeces. Alpacas are shorn for their fleece, annually in the case of **huacayas** and every two years for **suris** in the UK.

They are too large to **shear** like a sheep and are strapped down. This prevents them from struggling and getting cut. It also means the process is very quickly over and therefore not unduly stressful.

The **fleece** needs to be sorted before any processing can be done. The best part is over the body of the animal and is called the **blanket.**

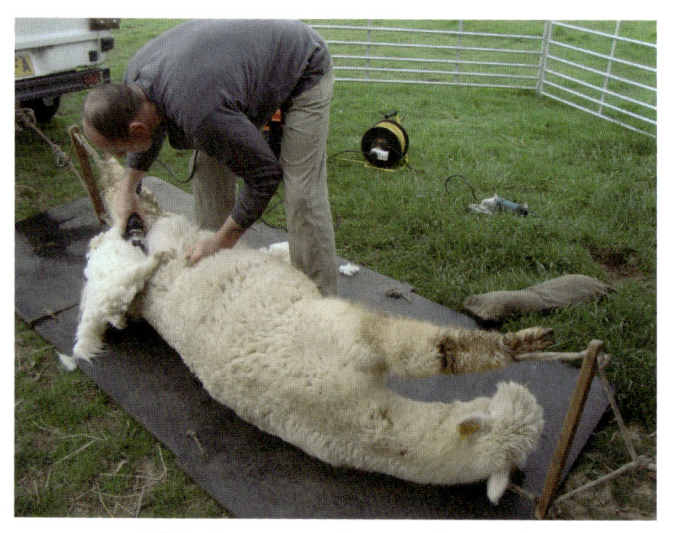

This is Aurora being sheared.

Off with the blanket!

Living with alpacas — 18

Summertime!

Although the native home of alpacas can reach very low temperatures, it can also be quite warm. Alpacas enjoy the sunshine and when it is warm and dry they will enjoy a good roll in the dust and, even more, they will enjoy a relaxing sunbathe!

Here is a very sleepy, sunbathing Micah.

Sometimes when you look across the field it might appear that several animals are unwell and stretched, flat out on the ground. The most likely thing is a nice doze in the sun.

Before **shearing** they must feel quite hot and will sometimes even try to paddle in the water trough!

Living with alpacas — 19

Wintertime!

Alpacas are from the altiplano in South America. The temperatures there can reach sub-zero temperatures as low as -20°C. The cold is less of a problem for alpacas than rain as they are very well insulated in their wonderful, warm fleeces. They have more trouble with wet as their fleeces don't contain the same oils as sheep to shed the water. Any snow we usually have is manageable for them. They are happy to be out in it but as grazing is not as easy, depending how deeply covered the grass is, they will eat more hay than at other times. Shelter must be available to alpacas all year round but they mostly choose not to use it, preferring to be outside.

Much less snow than the high mountains of the Andes,
but quite a lot for Devon!

Living with alpacas

What's it all for?

In the Uk alpacas are not bred for anything other than their **fibre**. This is a particularly soft, well insulated and strong natural **fibre**. It can be used for many things. A lot of breeders will work hard with their own fleeces to produce things that they can sell. They might sell things on their website, at craft fairs or farmers markets, or they might have the space to set up a 'farm shop' near their animals. It is especially nice for the customer to see the animals that produced the **fibre**.

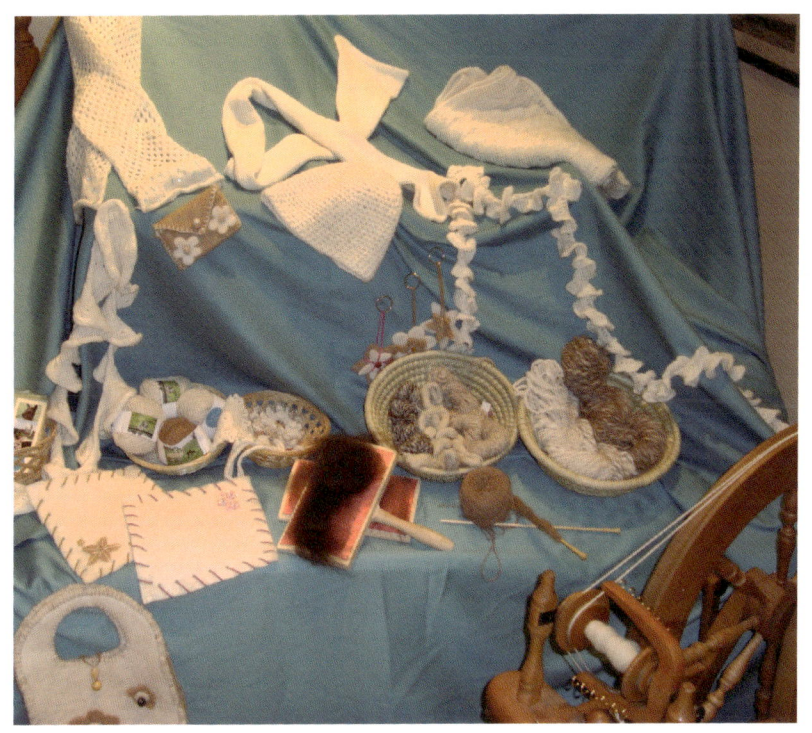

These are some of the things that go on my stalls. All made from our own lovely fibre.

Fibre can be hand spun or sent to a mill to be made into yarn for knitting or weaving into clothes, blankets and any number of items. It can also be made into felt to sew into other products. Fleece that hasn't been made into anything can even be cleaned and used as a filling for duvets or pet beds! The list could go on and is only limited by the imagination of the producer!

Living with alpacas — 21

Alpaca Facts

- Alpacas originate from South America.
- They produced the **fibres** worn by kings and throughout history they were highly revered by the native South Americans.
- The invasion by the Spaniards saw these beautiful animals being destroyed in vast numbers. Fortunately they survived, as a species, to tell the tale.
- Alpacas are one of the members of the South American Camelid family. This group includes alpacas, llamas, guanacos and vicunas. They are also related to camels.
- There are two types of alpaca. They are called **huacayas** and **suris**.
- **Huacayas** are the ones that look rather more 'fuzzy' and teddy-bear-like.
- **Suris** have longer locks of fleece which are rather like tassels or dreadlocks.
- Alpacas need other alpacas to live with. They are a herd animal and can become very lonely and even ill if kept without other alpaca friends.
- Alpacas are now being bred around the world for their wonderful **fibre**. It feels extremely soft to wear and has tremendous insulating properties.

- Alpaca **fibre** is different to sheep's wool in that it is usually finer and softer. It also contains no lanolin, which is the oil in sheep's wool that some people can be allergic to.
- Alpacas are becoming more popular for breeding in the UK.
- Females are pregnant for between 10 $\frac{1}{2}$ months and 12 months. The female is called a **hembra**. The male is called a **macho**.
- Alpacas will nearly always give birth to a single **cria**. Twins are very rare and it is even more rare for twins to survive.
- Alpacas will usually give birth during the day and without assistance.
- Alpacas are sometimes used as guards for sheep or chickens as they can help to keep foxes away. Females will see them as a threat to their young and males seem to see them as a good sport!
- Alpacas will live for about 15 to 20 years and a females might give birth to up to 15 **crias**.
- Alpacas measure approximately 90cm to their shoulders and 150cm to the top of their heads.
- Females will be big enough to breed between 12 and 18 months of age and males at about 2 $\frac{1}{2}$ years.
- The main noise an alpaca makes is a soft hum.
- When feeling threatened and wanting to be heard by the rest of the herd alpacas make an alarm call. This is quite a squeal and sounds a little like a bird screeching.

Glossary

Blanket — The name of the larger piece of fleece off the body of the alpaca.

Calve — Give birth to a young animal

Cria — The name of a baby alpaca

Crimp — The wave that runs along each fibre within the fleece

Cush — Sitting position of resting alpacas with all four legs tucked underneath them.

Fibre — What the fleece is made of and what is used to make beautiful products.

Gestation — The time for which a female is pregnant, from mating to giving birth.

Huacaya — The type of alpaca that looks woolly like a teddy bear.

Hembra — Female alpaca

Macho — Male alpaca

Ruminant — An animal that chews the cud

Rickets — Disease with softening and deformity of the bones, caused by too little vitamin D

Shearing — The removal of the years growth of fleece.

Staple length — The length of the fibre from the skin to the tip.

Suri — The type of alpaca thast has a fleece resembling tassles or dreadlocks.

Index

Andes 10, 20
baby 8, 10, 12, 24
birth 10, 11, 23, 24
calving 14
cria 8, 10, 11, 12, 14, 16, 23, 24
cud 8, 9, 24
cush 9, 24
diet 7
diseases 5, 24
fibre 5, 15, 17, 21, 22, 23, 24
fleece 17, 18, 20, 21, 22, 24
food 7, 8, 24
gestation 10, 24
grass 7, 20
grazing 7, 8, 20

hay 7, 8, 20
health 5, 8
hembra 23, 24
herd 9, 10, 12, 22, 23, 26
injections 5, 6, 9
macho 23, 24
mating 24
milk 12
orphan 12, 13
pregnancy 14
ruminant 8, 24
shelter 20
South America 6, 20, 22
vaccination 5
water 7, 19, 20
weaning 12
weight 5

Living with alpacas — 25

About the Author

Jane lives on the edge of Dartmoor in Devon with her three daughters, her dogs, rabbits, chickens and, of course, her alpacas. She and her husband used to work as primary school teachers but when he died she wanted to learn something new. She found out all about alpacas and found these beautiful, gentle, curious animals to be the perfect new job! She started breeding her own alpacas and enjoys introducing people to her herd. She also produces things from their fleeces and likes to have school children to visit.
You can find out what is happening at the moment by looking on www.tudorcottagealpacas.co.uk

"A well written and informative book on Alpaca farming in Devon. Hopefully this will inspire a future generation of Alpaca farmers."
Deborah Cunningham B.Vet.Med MRCVS

"Our children have really enjoyed learning about alpacas from 'Living with Alpacas' and it fired their imagination so that they asked lots of questions - luckily the book answered most of them as we read on! It is an interesting book on its own but can also be used in the classroom to support pupils' learning"
Heather Poustie, Headteacher

LaVergne, TN USA
21 October 2010
201774LV00002B